THE OTHER HALF OF HISTORY

THE OTHER HALF OF HISTORY

WOMEN

IN

MEDIEVAL

TIMES

Fiona Macdonald

EDRICK BOOKS

oup

First published in the United States of America in 2000
by Peter Bedrick Books
a division of NTC/Contemporary Publishing Group
4255 West Touhy Avenue
Lincolnwood (Chicago), Illinois 60712–1975, U.S.A.

Text copyright © Fiona Macdonald 2000
Copyright © Belitha Press Ltd 2000

Series editor: Claire Edwards
Series designer: Jamie Asher
Designer: Zoe Quayle
Picture researcher: Diana Morris
Consultant: Kate Moorse

Printed and bound in Hong Kong

Library of Congress Cataloging-in-Publication Data
is available from the United States Library of Congress.

Picture acknowledgments:
AAA Collection/© Ronald Sheridan: 42t, 45t.
AKG London: 1,16, 37,43b /Erich Lessing: front cover
l & r, 7br, 21b, 35b. Ashmolean Museum, Oxford/
Bridgeman Art Library: 20t. Biblioteca de El Escorial/
Bridgeman Art Library: 24 /ET Archive: 18l, 22b.
Biblioteca Estense, Modena/ET Archive: 26c.
Biblioteca Medicea-Laurenziana, Florence/Bridgeman
Art Library: 30t. Bibliothèque de l'Arsenal, Paris/ET
Archive: 21t. Bibliothèque National, Paris/AKG
London: 4bl, 10 /Bridgeman Art Library: 3c, 7bl, 17t,
29t, 30b /ET Archive: 6, 43c. Bibliothèque
Ste. Geneviève, Paris/Bridgeman Art Library: 15b.
Bodleian Library, Oxford: 5tr, 12b. The British Library,
London/ Bridgeman Art Library: back cover l, 5bl, 9l,
11t, 17b, 18t, 20r, 22c, 23b, 25b, 26b, 27b, 31c, 34c,
35t, 40, 42b, 45b /ET Archive: 19, 44t.

Picture acknowledgments cont.:
Castello del Buonconsiglio, Trent/Bridgeman Art
Library: front cover c, 32c. Corpus Christi College,
Cambridge: 36c. C. M. Dixon: 8, 13b, 25t, 29b, 38.
Ecole des Beaux Arts, Paris/Bridgeman Art Library: 16t.
Fitzwilliam Museum, Cambridge/Bridgeman Art
Library: back cover r, 28b. Isabella Stewart Gardener
Museum, Boston, MA/Bridgeman Art Library: 41b.
Sonia Halliday & Laura Lushington: 39t. Issogne
Castle, Valle d'Aosta/Bridgeman Art Library: 31b.
Musée de l'Assistance Publique, Paris/ET Archive: 34b.
Musée Condé, Chantilly/Giraudon/Bridgeman Art
Library: 3cl, 7t, 14, 15t, 27t, 32b/ET Archive: 44t.
Musée de Cluny/C. M. Dixon: 23c. Museo Bargello,
Florence/
ET Archive: 3cr, 12c. National Library of Scotland,
Edinburgh/Bridgeman Art Library: 3r, 11b.
Osterreichisches Staatsbibliothek, Vienna/Bridgeman
Art Library: 28t. El Prado, Madrid/Bridgeman Art
Library: 41t. Private Collection/Bridgeman Art Library
33c, 39b. San Francisco, Assisi/ET Archive: 37t.
Sta. Maria della Scala Hospital, Sienna/ET Archive: 13t
V & A Museum, London/ET Archive: 3l, 4c, 9br. Dea
& Chapter of Westminster: 33b.

The quotation on page 36, top right, is from FRANCIS
AND CLARE translation and introduction by Regis J.
Armstrong, O.F.M. CAP. And Ignatius C. Brady, O.F.M.
© 1982 by Paulist Press, Inc. Use by permission of
Paulist Press.

CONTENTS

SETTING THE SCENE

Medieval Europe

This book looks at women's lives in Europe from around AD 1000 to 1500. This period is often called the Middle Ages or the medieval era, but these names were never used by people living at that time. They were invented by historians about 300 years ago. From about AD 1000 a rich civilization developed in Europe. It combined the laws and customs of Roman, Celtic, German, Slav and Viking cultures and was based on a powerful Christian faith.

Nobles and priests
Kings, nobles, and leaders of the Christian Church were at the top of medieval society. They were very rich and powerful—and almost all men. Kings made laws, with advice from parliaments, and led armies into battle. Male government officials, merchants and lawyers also played an important part in public life. The Church made its own laws, and ran schools and universities.

> Very learned men say that Nature always aims to produce perfection. Therefore, if it were possible, Nature would produce only men. When a woman is born, this is a mistake or imperfection....
>
> BALDASSARE CASTIGLIONE
> (WRITTEN IN 1528, LOOKING BACK
> AT THE MIDDLE AGES)

Women from ordinary families worked alongside their husbands and fathers in the fields.

Peasant farmers
Most people in medieval Europe were peasants. They worked as laborers for rich lords on their great estates. In return they were allowed to farm small pieces of land to grow food for their families. Many lords had the right to collect taxes from their peasants. Some peasant men and women were not free to leave their lord's land.

A baby prince is carried by his mother in a procession through Paris. Noblewomen were valued as mothers of future kings, heiresses of rich fathers and wives of rulers.

A living from the land

How people farmed depended on where they lived. In northern lands such as Scandinavia, where the climate was harsh, farmers grew crops such as rye and oats. They kept sheep and goats, and went hunting and fishing for food. In warmer southern lands, such as Italy and Spain, wheat, grapes and olives grew well. After about 1200, towns and cities throughout Europe began to grow rich through trade. European merchants and scholars traveled long distances by land and sea to make contacts with people in distant lands.

The Italian trading port of Venice was one of Europe's richest cities. Merchants from Venice traded with Asia and the Middle East.

Multicultural

Most men and women in medieval Europe belonged to the Christian Church. But there was also a powerful and cultured Muslim kingdom in southern Spain, and communities of Jewish people in many European towns. Until the end of medieval times, there were also groups of pagan peoples living along Europe's northeastern frontiers.

Jewish women sweep away crumbs of bread made with yeast before the festival of the Passover, as part of a religious ritual.

Castles and Cathedrals

Many wonderful works of art made in medieval Europe still survive today. But how much do they tell us about medieval women's lives? Medieval people were great artists and craftworkers. They built castles and cathedrals, made beautiful manuscripts and paintings and glittering jewelry. But most of these were made by men. Few women had the chance to train as artists. Sometimes, the wives or daughters of male artists were taught at home, and a few women, employed as servants in workshops, learned useful craft skills.

A fifteenth-century woman paints a self-portrait. On her left there are jars of paint. On her right there are tools for carving wooden picture frames.

I know a woman painter called Anastasia. She is so clever and skilled at painting backgrounds and borders of manuscripts that there is no better artist in the whole of Paris [France] —where all the best artists live.

CHRISTINE DE PISAN (1364–1430)

Lost works

The names of a few women artists and craftworkers have survived, such as Anastasia from France (described above) and Sancia from Spain, who made a beautiful silver cross, and signed it with her name. We also know the names of many women famous for fine needlework. Sewing of all kinds was traditionally a female skill, but cloth does not last as long as silver or stone, and many women's works of art have crumbled away.

Image or reality

Many medieval paintings and statues show women of different kinds, from peasant girls to queens or saints. The details of these works give us information about women in medieval times, but we need to study them carefully. Most works of art were created by professional artists. They did not aim to paint or carve a simple record of what they saw. Instead they aimed to create a fashionable image, or to send a special religious or political message through their work.

Women were here

At first sight, some of the most famous medieval buildings seem to tell us little about women's lives. But women are often shown on tombs and memorials in churches and cathedrals. Some are remembered for giving money to pay for works of art such as stained glass windows or embroidered altar-cloths. In recent years, archaeologists have discovered that many medieval castles had separate living quarters for women, where they could enjoy privacy away from rowdy soldiers. Some castles even had private gardens where women could enjoy the fresh air away from men.

Medieval artists often painted women as abstract figures, such as Justice or Jealousy. Here the woman spinning the wheel represents Fortune.

Skilled needlewomen used silk and gold and silver thread to decorate belts, gloves, robes and cushions with patterns and pictures.

This stone carving from Naumberg cathedral in Germany is of Uta von Ballenstedt. She gave money to help build the cathedral in about AD 1000.

Hidden from History

Compared with many other past civilizations, there is plenty of written evidence to tell us about medieval times. But most writings are by men about men and their world. Men who wrote about women were often very critical of them, as you can see from the complaint by a medieval woman, right.

Through men's eyes

Only a few people in medieval Europe could read and write, and most of them were men. This means that much of the information about women is presented from a man's point of view. There is very little writing about the daily activities that filled most women's everyday lives.

Legal documents

Government documents, such as those describing who owned land and paid taxes, usually deal only with men, because men earned more money, and owned most land. Records of law courts describe the activities of male lawyers and witnesses. Women, especially married women, did not often appear in court in an active role. But historians carefully study all written documents and collect tiny details of women's lives. By piecing them together they create a clearer picture of the past.

Unreal and unfair?

Men wrote about many different kinds of women in poems and stories. They range from bloodthirsty battle heroines, to sweet and pretty lovers, or wicked wives. But these images of women tell us more about men's fears and fantasies, and fashions in reading, than about real women's lives. They give us some evidence of the past, but we cannot rely on them as accurate descriptions.

Rich medieval women who could not write hired scribes and clerks to write letters and other documents for them. Here a woman is dictating to a man, who is writing in a book.

Written by women

We can find out more about women from other sorts of written evidence, created by women themselves. There are letters, and prayer books, religious texts, diaries, medical books, collections of accounts, all written or dictated by women. There are also honest descriptions of real women, written by sympathetic or admiring men. There are even many poems, songs and plays written by women. These were enjoyed by everyone—so much so, that men often claimed to have written them.

Christine de Pisan (see page 45) was the most famous woman writer of medieval times. This painting shows her working at her desk.

The pages (right) from a Book of Hours were made for a noblewoman called Margaret de Foix in about 1470. Noblewomen often paid for books of prayers and holy writings to be made for them.

PROUD POET

To end these stories that I've told
And translated from other languages,
I'll tell you my name, so you'll remember me.
It's Marie, and I come from France.
Now it may well be that some male writer
Will try to pretend my work is his.
But I'm not having that!
I'm no fool—I don't want to be forgotten!

This is part of a poem by Marie de France, a women poet who lived around 1180. We know little about her, except her name, which she recorded in the lines quoted above. Unlike many other women writers of her time, she did not want to hide from public view. Instead, she announced her name proudly, and warned any man against claiming to be the author of her works.

Reading tastes

Some historians have suggested that by the end of the Middle Ages educated women had developed particular tastes in reading. The evidence comes from the fact that many women left books to other women in their wills. These included books for teaching children to read, recipes for medicines, and poems and romances.

WOMEN AND SOCIETY

Women's Status

Legally, women were treated like children—unable to take part in many important activities open to men, and always guided by and obedient to men. In about 1180 one English lawyer wrote, "Every married woman is a sort of infant." In one sense, he was right. In the eyes of the law, most women never grew up.

> Women should obey their men.... It it is natural that those who are less important should serve those who are more important.... Women have no right to power. Let them obey men in everything. Women should not teach, or be a witness, or give a guarantee, or be a judge....
>
> GRATIAN, A CHURCH LAWYER, WHO LIVED IN ITALY IN ABOUT 1140

No chance to learn
Women were not allowed to follow any interesting, well-paid careers. They could not go to university, which might qualify them to be doctors, lawyers or priests. They could not join the army, the navy or work for the government. They could not be judges, serve on juries, or be witnesses to official documents. Although many powerful women played an important part in politics, by advising their husbands and brothers, or by building up a network of powerful friends, they could not be chosen to represent the community at councils or parliaments.

This assembly of powerful landowners and lawyers was called to meet King Charles VII of France in 1458. Women could not take part in important decision-making meetings like this.

Bound by the law

The law allowed women little freedom to control their lives. A woman could not marry without her parents' consent, could not usually own property (though she could share her husband's), run her own business without permission, have legal control of her children, or get a divorce (except in unusual circumstances). In many countries a woman could not inherit land from her father, unless she had no brothers.

Good behavior

Unwritten rules of good behavior shaped many women's lives. These rules were especially important for rich or noble women, who had to create the right impression of elegance and self-control in public. They could not take trips, or visit shops, inns or markets on their own, but had to be accompanied by at least one servant. They could not spend time alone with any man, unless he was their husband, father, brother, or a priest. They were not expected to express their views freely, or laugh loudly, or swear. They were supposed to speak quietly. They could not do anything their families disapproved of—from wearing the latest fashions to reading unsuitable books. Few of these unwritten rules applied to boys or men.

Although women could not train for professional careers, many ordinary women did work as servants and laborers. Here Italian men and women workers are lining up to be paid.

This Scottish noblewoman's dress is decorated with her husband's and father's coats of arms. Married women had no status of their own, but shared the rank of their closest male relative.

Women as Wives

Almost all women expected to get married. Because women were not equal with men by law, and because they were always paid less for working, it was very difficult for an unmarried woman to survive. Some churchmen taught that marriage should be a partnership, but even so, husbands were seen as the head of the partnership.

This ivory decoration shows two lovers meeting. Medieval people recognized love's power, even though marriages were often not based on shared love. Many poems and songs tell stories of wives who fall in love with other men. Most do not have a happy ending.

The importance of love

Marriage was the single most important event in a woman's life. It affected her place in society, her wealth, her lifestyle and her hopes of happiness. But many medieval women were not free to choose who they married, or when their marriage took place. The richer or more noble they were, the more likely their family was to choose a husband for them. No one thought it was important for the couple to be in love, or even to like one another. What mattered was each family's rank, wealth and political power.

A bride and her bridesmaids (below) walk to a church, accompanied by musicians and other guests. The groom, his relatives and a priest wait by the church door.

At this Italian wedding, a newly married couple exchange rings as a public sign that they are bound to one another. They are surrounded by friends and family, but there is no priest.

Marriage market

Among wealthy people, marriages were like business deals. They were arranged to increase a family's riches, or make alliances with other important people. On marriage, the bride's parents gave the groom's family a dowry. This could mean valuable property or land. In return, the groom's family promised to provide the bride with a dower. This was a lifetime's share in her husband's property if he died. Boys, as well as girls, had to agree to arranged marriages. But young noblemen (before and after marriage) were allowed to choose girlfriends, while young noblewomen were kept carefully guarded at home.

Until the end of the Middle Ages, people did not have to be married in a church. A public commitment by the couple was all that was needed. Even so, most medieval marriages did take place in church. The couple arrived at the church door, dressed in their best clothes and accompanied by family and friends. Here they declared they were man and wife. Then they moved inside the church for prayers and a blessing.

Afterward, there was a feast, with music and dancing, sometimes followed by special ceremonies to escort the newly married couple to bed. In southern Europe, the bridegroom's friends ran around the streets after the wedding, making a lot of noise. They threatened to keep the new couple awake all night unless the bridegroom gave them money or other gifts.

Engaged couples sometimes had their portraits painted as a record of their promise to marry one another. This painting from a plate shows a young couple and an artist, who is painting their portrait on another plate.

13

Freedom to choose

Girls from ordinary families were more likely to be able to choose their own partners than those from rich families. Unlike noble girls, they were allowed out of the house alone, to run errands, or work as servants or in the fields. They came into contact with married and unmarried men that way. But even so, most ordinary girls and boys needed their parents' approval for a marriage. Without this, they could not hope to inherit family workshops or land.

You owe love and fidelity to your husbands ... whether they are young or old, good or bad, peaceful or fond of arguments, loyal or unfaithful. You should behave well and wisely toward them, whoever they are, and keep your promise to be faithful and loyal to them, keeping control of your temper at all times and always doing your duty.

CHRISTINE DE PISAN (1364–1430)

A loving wife kneels in prayer by her dying husband's bedside. A good wife looked after her husband while he was well and nursed him when he was sick. She also prayed for him while he was alive and after he had died.

North and south

In southern Europe, girls from ordinary families married very young (12 was the minimum age in Church law). Their husbands were often around 15 years older, with much greater experience of life and work. This could make marriage partnerships very unequal. It was hard for a young girl to have any influence if her husband was almost twice her age. In northern Europe, ordinary women often did not get married until they were in their mid to late twenties. Their husbands were usually around the same age, although no one thought it strange if a husband was much older.

Married young

Girls from wealthy families were betrothed (legally engaged) in childhood, and married young—often before they were 16 years old. Parents wanted to secure the marriage alliance they had planned as soon as possible. The husband might be much younger or much older than the bride.

Staying together

Most marriages lasted until one of the partners died. Church laws, which governed marriage, made it very difficult for a woman to get a divorce, even if her husband was violent or unfaithful. But men could turn their wives out into the street with nothing at all if they discovered that they had been unfaithful. It was also easy for unhappily married men to abandon their wives and children. Unlike women, it was acceptable for men to wander the streets alone, or seek shelter in an alehouse. It was easy for them to find work far from home, by joining the army, enlisting as a sailor, hiding in a big city, or just wandering from farm to farm doing seasonal work. A popular medieval saying tended to blame women when this happened: "Three things drive a man away from home—a smoking chimney, a leaking roof and a nagging wife."

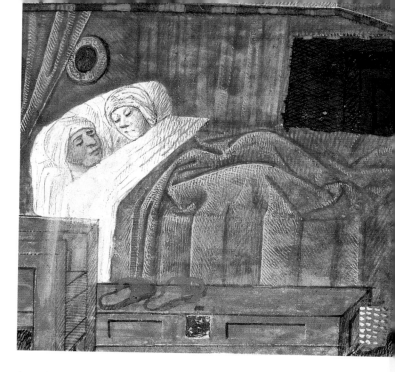

We do not know how many medieval marriages worked out well. But this picture of an elderly couple in bed seems to have a feeling of peace and companionship.

Obedience

The law expected women to obey their husbands, and allowed men to beat their wives for being lazy or disobedient, although they were not allowed to injure them seriously. Medieval women hoped for happiness in marriage, but knew they might not always find it. They had been taught since childhood that duty and loyalty and a roof over their head were more important than love.

Some women suffered from their husband's violent temper even if they had done nothing wrong. Here a jealous husband beats his wife, because he thinks she has been seeing another man.

15

Mothers and Children

Motherhood was women's most important work—at least in the eyes of men. Although medieval women were second-class citizens, they were honored as mothers by medieval writers because they gave birth to boys.

Motherhood

On the average, medieval families were not large. Rich women might be pregnant six times, but have only four surviving children. A peasant might be pregnant three or four times and have two surviving children. Rich women had more children because they married younger, were better fed, and employed wet nurses to feed their babies. Peasant women sometimes went hungry, did tiring work, and breastfed their babies for about two years. This meant they were less likely to become pregnant quickly again.

In this family scene, a wife keeps her husband company in his workshop. Their son is tidying up the wood shavings from the floor.

Caring for children

Medieval women behaved very differently with their children, depending on whether they were rich or poor. A rich woman saw little of her children, especially when they were small, but arranged for them to be looked after (see box). A poor woman had to keep a careful watch over her children all the time. Medieval villages and towns were dangerous places, with open fires, dee wells and ditches, and wandering animals. At night she had to get up to feed her children or soothe their cries.

Ordinary women had to combine child care with many other tasks. This stained glass window shows a mother spinning wool and rocking her baby's cradle at the same time.

These teenage girls (front left) are brushing wool fibers and smoothing them with wire combs. Most young girls were expected to know how to spin and weave cloth. Many girls from ordinary families made all their own clothes.

NURSEMAIDS

Like a mother, a child's nursemaid feels happy when the baby she cares for is happy, and suffers when he suffers. She picks him up when he falls, feeds him when he cries, and comforts him when he is ill.... She bounces him on her hands, shoulders and knees.... Humming and singing, she strokes him as he sleeps....

FROM A THIRTEENTH-CENTURY ENCYCLOPEDIA

Mothers from wealthy families did not look after their babies themselves, but hired nursemaids (as above) to care for them. But the encyclopedia entry also tells us how medieval mothers must have cared for their own babies. Many medieval women had to cope with feelings of grief and loss when their babies died. Historians think that about one in five babies died before they reached the age of five.

Education

Girls were educated at home by their mothers, or by tutors if they lived in rich households. Girls from ordinary families learned practical household skills, such as cooking, cleaning, looking after animals and babies, and nursing. They were encouraged to work hard and develop common sense. Wealthy girls learned to read and maybe also to write, do fine embroidery, and sing or play a musical instrument. They were taught stories from the Bible, and perhaps also some history and poetry. Most important of all, girls from rich families learned how to behave in society. They learned what sort of clothes to wear, how to walk and talk, and how to be polite to everyone they met.

This medieval drawing shows a mother and father carrying young boys on their shoulders. The children seem to be trying to have a fight.

Widowhood

There were two main groups of women who lived without men in medieval Europe. The first was religious women such as nuns, who chose to dedicate their lives to God (see pages 34–37). The second group was widows. Because many men died before they reached old age, in war, in accidents at work, or from diseases, many women became widows, often by the time they were 40 years old. Early death meant that few medieval marriages lasted for a long time.

Women left alone proved that they were able to run houses and estates without men. This picture shows a noblewoman giving orders to her female gardener.

This portrait of a widow is from a Spanish manuscript. Her bowed head, clasped hands and cloak wrapped closely around her show her sadness at the loss of her husband.

Greedy or pitiful?

Medieval male writers seemed to hold different views about widows. On the one hand, some said widows should be helped and pitied; on the other hand, others described them as greedy for land and money, and desperate for love. There was a reason for these opposite opinions. A widow's life could be comfortable and free, or very miserable indeed. This depended on whether she was rich or poor. For rich women, widowhood was the only time in their lives when they could own property, decide how to spend money, entertain their own friends, and bring up their children in the way they chose. But for poor women without a house, land or money, widowhood was a struggle to survive.

Poor widows

By law, a widow could choose whether she married again after her husband died. Many poor women remarried simply to find somewhere to live and someone to help feed their children. In wartime, rich or poor widows might marry to gain a man's protection from armies attacking their lands.

Rich widows

Rich women often had little freedom to stay single. If they had inherited a large estate from their dead husband, they were put under great pressure by their families, or by the king, to marry again. in England, the law gave the king the right to collect a large sum of money from anyone who wanted to marry a noble widow. Sometimes rich women were kidnapped and forcibly married to men who wanted to get hold of their lands.

FAIR SHARES AND GOOD BEHAVIOR

Usually a widow was allowed a share of her dead husband's property during her lifetime, plus one-third of his goods. This could cause problems if a man died leaving a very young widow with baby sons. As the sons grew up and married, they might resent the fact that their mother had the right to enjoy so much of the family property. Husbands often made wills to make sure that their widows would be treated fairly.

For example, in 1518 a wool worker named John Neele made a will leaving his son all the tools of his trade, plus a shop and a room in his house. He added that his son could only have these things if he was kind to his mother. If not, she should shut him out of the house for the rest of her life.

Marriage or the Church

The Church encouraged widows not to remarry, and offered a woman legal protection if she decided to become a vowess—someone who promised to live the rest of her life without men in order to become closer to God. Many vowesses lived in their family home, but homeless widows who wanted to stay single might go to live in religious communities, where they were supported by charity.

Some rich widows enjoyed life surrounded by female friends. Young male poets and musicians often asked such women to be their patrons. They wrote poems or songs in return for food, clothes and money.

HEALTH AND BEAUTY

Changing Fashions

From a father's advice (right), we know that fashions changed in medieval times. But most women were expected to dress modestly, and to wear clothes that covered them from head to toe.

Medieval women wore brooches, like the one above in the shape of a bird, to fasten their clothes.

Peasant women throughout Europe wore simple clothes like these: a kerchief, a long robe and leather boots. This farmworker also has a purse hanging from her belt.

Modesty
There were many local styles in different parts of Europe, but most medieval women wore a similar costume made up of a long, loose shift with a long robe and perhaps a sleeveless tunic or apron on top. Shifts were usually made of linen. Rich women wore robes of fine wool dyed in brilliant colors, or of velvet and satin embroidered with silk, jewels and gold thread. Poor women wore robes of homespun wool, which they may have made themselves.

Keeping warm
In cold weather women wore a long thick cloak—lined with fur if they could afford it. Poor women went barefoot, but everyone else wore knee-length woolen stockings and leather shoes or boots. A girdle (long belt) and shoulder brooches, or simple pins, kept all these clothes in place.

Changing fashions
Toward the end of the Middle Ages, fashions changed. Young women at royal courts throughout Europe wore revealing, low-cut robes with very full skirts and trains. Men wore tight leggings and short tunics. Another new style was wavy, ragged borders on sleeves and cloaks. Church leaders complained that these fashions were indecent, immoral and a waste of expensive material.

In the fifteenth century, wealthy women and men dressed in daring fashions. The women wore low necklines and the men wore short tunics.

Crowning glory

Women did not cut their hair, because long hair was a sign of beauty. Unmarried girls wore braids, or left their hair hanging loose. They might wear a headscarf, ribbons or a headband (jeweled, if they were rich). For special occasions, girls wove garlands of flowers to wear in their hair.

Respectable hair

Married women covered their hair at all times. Older women, religious women, and women who wanted to be thought respectable wore kerchiefs of plain white linen, though they often were careful to choose the very best fabric, and to arrange it in the most flattering style.

This carving shows a woman wearing a wide band of cloth, covering from her forehead to her chin. The style, called a wimple, was popular with married women from about 1000 to 1300, and was worn by nuns all through the Middle Ages.

She wore a deep blue cloak that fastened around the neck. It had precious stones all the way down the front. She also wore a necklace of glass beads, and a hood made of black lambskin and lined with the fur of white cats.... Around her waist she wore a belt of touchwood [a kind of fungus] with a big purse hanging from it. This was where she stored her magic charms. On her feet she wore shoes made of hairy calfskin, fastened with thongs and with big tin buttons. She had catskin gloves, lined with white fur....

We don't know the woman's name or who wrote this description of her. But she lived in Greenland in the eleventh century and was famous for being able to see into the future. Her clothes are warm and show her high status.

Fashionable headdresses

Rich, fashionable, young married women arranged their hair to frame their faces, and covered it with nets made of silk or gold thread. At the end of the Middle Ages, huge headdresses made of cloth and padded with horsehair became fashionable in towns and at court.

Beauty aids

Although Church leaders disapproved, some women painted their faces with makeup made from fruits, flowers, soil and animal fat. After about 1370 they also plucked hair from their eyebrows and foreheads to create a fashionable barefaced look.

Women's Bodies

Women's bodies were not seen as their own in medieval times. Women spent their lives under male guardianship—first their father and then their husband. This offered them protection from attack in violent times. But it also meant that they were watched and guarded, to make sure they did not get close to men.

Respectable women were not allowed to travel alone. They always traveled with a male relative or trusted family friend, or an older woman. Sometimes a group of younger women could also act as guardians.

A faithful wife

Men had a very important reason for wanting to control women's bodies. Fathers felt it was their duty to make sure that their daughters stayed virgins until they were married. Husbands needed to feel sure that their lands would be inherited by their own sons. The only way they could be certain of this was by making sure that their wives did not sleep with other men and have children by them.

Beautiful and deadly

The Church taught that women could be dangerous. Their beauty and behavior might tempt men to sin, as Eve had tempted Adam in the Bible. One scholar taught that women were "the gateway to hell." Doctors claimed that women were less able than men to control their feelings. They needed to be controlled, for their own good.

This page from a book of Bible stories shows Adam and Eve covering themselves with fig leaves. The Church taught that after Eve had tempted Adam to sin, being naked was sinful.

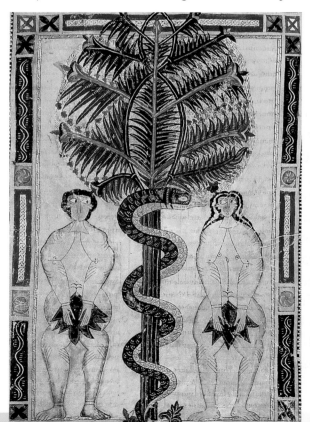

Purity for God

The Church also taught that the best way of life was to remain unmarried, and a virgin. That way, people could devote more time and thought to God. Being married was second-best, but most medieval people did marry. The Church taught that living together without being married was a sin.

In medieval times, purity was one of the most valued virtues. In stories, magical creatures called unicorns were symbols of purity. Only virgins could catch them. This tapestry shows a woman and a pure white unicorn.

Views on women

Despite the attitude of men such as Odo of Cluny (see quotation), most men in medieval Europe did not hate women and liked to spend time in their company. They admired women's intelligence, patience, helpfulness and gentleness. When their experience of real women combined with the Church's teachings, some men were not quite sure what to think. Their confused view of women is reflected in many poems and songs, and in laws that treated women as worthy of respect, but morally inferior to men.

THE VIRGIN MARY

According to the Bible, Eve (the first woman) tempted Adam (the first man) to disobey God's commands. This was what caused pain and suffering in the world. But the Church taught that another woman, the Virgin Mary, helped repair the damage Eve had done, by giving birth to Jesus, God's only son. Jesus came to save the world, and to free people from sin and suffering.

For medieval men and women the Virgin Mary was the ideal woman. She was obedient to God, was a devoted wife and mother and (miraculously) was still a virgin. Church leaders taught that women should try to follow her example in their own lives.

This painting shows the Angel Gabriel telling the Virgin Mary that she will give birth to Jesus.

Sickness and Health

The description of pregnancy (right) comes from a religious text telling women to stay virgins. It paints a gloomy picture of pregnancy, but it highlights the fact that pregnancy and childbirth were the most dangerous times in a medieval woman's life. Many women died giving birth, and diseases linked to childbearing caused suffering for women years after their baby had been born.

> *Your pink, healthy face will become thin, and turn sickly green like grass; your eyes will lose their sparkle.... Your belly will swell out, you will have indigestion and stitches in your side. Your back will ache.... You will look pale and ill—no longer beautiful. You will have a bitter taste in your mouth, and everything you eat will make you feel sick.... You will be unable to sleep at night, because you will worry so much about labor pains....*
>
> FROM A BOOK ENCOURAGING YOUNG WOMEN TO BECOME NUNS, BY A THIRTEENTH-CENTURY PRIEST

Women could not train as doctors, but they could be midwives. Here two midwives support a pregnant woman as she is about to give birth.

Doctors for the rich

How did women deal with ill health in medieval times? Like most things in medieval society, it depended on whether they were rich or poor. Rich families called in university-trained doctors. These were always men, because women could not go to universities. Professional male doctors relied on writings by ancient Greek scientists to guide them, and on more recent medical texts, mostly written by churchmen.

Nurses for the poor

Poor families could not afford to pay for doctors. They relied on traditional knowledge of herbal medicines and first aid. This was usually passed from woman to woman within a family. In many communities there was also a wise woman who made a special study of nursing skills and medicines. In towns, women (usually from poor families) worked as nurses in hospitals run by nuns, or cared for patients in their own homes.

Midwives

Women in childbirth relied on midwives to help them. Although midwives were not professionally qualified, some were very skilled. Toward the end of the Middle Ages, university-trained doctors tried to ban women from practicing any kind of medicine, even caring for mothers in childbirth. They accused women who used magic charms and ancient herbal remedies of witchcraft.

TROTULA

Trotula was famous in medieval times for writing a medical text. For a while some historians thought that Trotula never existed, but they have now discovered that she lived and worked in Salerno, Italy, in about 1200. Several books were signed with her name, but only one was written by her. The others were probably written by men who used her name because it was trusted and respected.

Trotula's book is mostly about women's illnesses. She makes use of medical information from several different sources. These included knowledge from ancient Greek and Arabic texts taught at universities. She also relied on her own firsthand observation of patients, and a traditional knowledge of plants and herbs.

Women giving birth often called to St. Margaret to help them. In legend, she was swallowed by a dragon but escaped from its belly unharmed. This carving shows St. Margaret and the dragon.

Healing herbs and lucky charms

Rich and poor women used lucky charms. They might use holy water from a church to sprinkle over a sick animal or child, or borrow the girdle of a woman saint to wear while giving birth. They made mixtures of herbs and spices to try and cure illness, to act as contraceptives or to help them become pregnant. One medieval woman wrote to her sister, recommending a herbal mixture to help her have children. But she added, "It stinks so much that there have been husbands who have thrown it away."

Women made beauty creams and healing ointments from animal fat and herbs. This manuscript shows a woman in her shop. It is stocked with mirrors, combs and ointments.

WOMEN AND WORK

Women in Villages

Most women in medieval Europe lived in the countryside and worked on farms. Women's work was essential to help the family survive. A peasant woman was admired if she was strong, energetic and practical.

... I get up early ... milk our cows and turn them into the field.... Then I make butter. ... Afterward I make cheese.... Then the children need looking after.... I give the chickens food ... and look after the young geese.... I bake, I brew.... I twist rope.... I tease out wool, and card it, and spin it on a wheel.... I organize food for the cattle, and for ourselves.... I look after all the household. ...

FROM A BALLAD (A POEM THAT TELLS A STORY) FIRST WRITTEN DOWN IN ABOUT 1500

Food, warmth, clothing

A housewife's main responsibilities were to provide food, warmth and clothing. It was her job to provide meals every day for her husband, children and any servants, and to make sure they had enough food in winter or if the harvest failed. She salted meat to preserve it, and made butter and cheese. She fetched water from the village well or stream, and brewed ale. She grew vegetables and herbs in her cottage garden. She crushed grain in a hand mill, or carried heavy sacks of it to the nearest windmill or water mill, where it could be ground into flour.

Women baked bread from wheat, oats or barley in little clay ovens at home, or carried it to the village bakehouse to be cooked. Here a woman is baking flat loaves over an open fire.

Peasant women cared for the family's chickens, sheep, goats and cows. Here a woman is feeding a mother hen and her chicks with grain. She carries a distaff for spinning wool under her arm

Hard labor

A peasant women often helped in the fields at plowing or harvest time. She might earn a little money by weeding crops in the fields. She had to gather firewood, clean out fires, and make candles from rushes and animal fat. She also had to keep the house clean using only cold water, hard soap, and a broom made of twigs.

Weaving and washing

A peasant woman also had to clean flax and wool and spin them into thread. Sometimes she might sell this to merchants in towns for a little extra money, or she might weave it into rough fabric and sew clothes for her family. She also had to keep her family's clothes clean and free of pests, such as lice and fleas. She rubbed them with strong-smelling herbs, and washed them, usually in the nearest stream. It was heavy work to wring the wet clothes out, and spread them over trees and bushes to dry. No wonder people said, "A woman's work is never done."

Rough wool had to be picked clean of twigs and insects, then carded (combed with stiff brushes) before it could be spun into thread. These women are carding wool (right) and spinning it on a wheel (left).

At harvest time wives worked with their husbands to gather the grain. The harvest would feed the family for the coming year.

Women's world

A housewife had a recognized position in the community. She was mistress of the household and ran the family home. In the daytime villages became a women's world. While men were out in the fields, women met and chatted as they carried out their daily chores. Some shared their work, or divided it among themselves. For example, a woman who was good at baking might exchange her loaves of bread with someone for fresh eggs or jugs of ale.

Working girls

As her name made clear, a housewife was a married woman. Unmarried women from ordinary families also worked hard, but they rarely had homes of their own. Most girls stayed in their parents' house until they were married. They helped with housework and baby care. They were sent to gather berries, mushrooms and honey, to look after sheep and goats, or to work at jobs such as haymaking and grape picking. Some earned money for their family by spinning and weaving. Unmarried girls like this were often described as their parents' servants.

On country estates, women with special skills, like this shepherdess, worked alongside men. Women who looked after sheep had to be tough to endure cold, wet nights outdoors at lambing time.

This peasant woman is carrying a heavy sack of grain to a water mill, where it will be ground into flour. In many villages, the lord of the manor had the right to make peasants use his mill—and charge them.

Leaving home

In countries where women married later, unmarried girls sometimes left home when they reached the age of about 14. They went to work as servants for wealthier peasant families, or in castles, manor houses or in towns. Servants had no personal freedom, but they did have some job security because they were usually hired on yearly contracts. Servants were given food, somewhere to live training in a skill such as housekeeping or cooking, and wages as well. Women servants usually earned lower wages than men, which was true of all women's work, but skilled servants were respected and valued by their employers.

Some women used their knowledge of preparing food to earn money. The woman on the right is making cheese in a small factory.

Saving for the future

Being a servant gave unmarried girls the chance to save up for household goods, such as storage chests or spinning wheels. These would be useful when they married and set up their own homes. Many girls also met their future husbands while they were away from home. These men were usually employed as servants by the same master and mistress, or at a nearby house, or as farmworkers or laborers.

A servant girl (far right) waits for orders, while her master and mistress eat. A young boy servant brings more food.

Women in Towns

Compared with country-dwellers, medieval women living in towns found a wide range of work to do. In a poem written in about 1380, an English writer describes a visit to a London tavern and the women he meets there who earn their living in the city. They include Beton, who brews beer and runs a tavern, Cesse, who makes shoes, Rose, who sells dishes, and Clarice and Pernelle, who are barmaids.

This picture shows women twisting strands of silk into thread, then winding it onto spools. It was painted to decorate a document recording the rules of the silk-weavers' guild in Florence, Italy.

Family firm

Towns were centers of craftwork and trade. A townswoman often worked in the family business, such as a craft workshop, or helped her merchant husband arrange business deals and keep accounts. Few women from merchant families traveled long distances abroad to buy and sell. But, especially in the great trading ports of Italy, they did sometimes employ sea captains and merchants to travel and trade overseas on their behalf.

Training and organization

Officially girls were not allowed to train as craftworkers, and women were not usually allowed to become members of craftworkers' guilds. But in some cities such as Rouen and Paris, in France, and Cologne, in Germany, women silkworkers formed guilds of their own, and appointed women officials to check production standards. In London, widows of male guild members were allowed to continue their husbands' businesses for the rest of their lives. Often, this meant that the women employed trained men to produce goods for them, while they managed the business and sold the finished products.

Some medieval women worked as sales clerks in shops. This French manuscript shows a woman selling jewelry to a wealthy male customer.

Women alone

Some women went into business on their own, as craftworkers or more often as shopkeepers. They worked under a special legal arrangement known as *femmes soles*, which is French for "women alone." This meant that their husbands would not have to pay their debts if their businesses lost money. This scheme gave women plenty of freedom, but it was also risky. Without a husband to back them, women could find it hard to survive if businesses went wrong.

Low-paid jobs

There were many other women working in towns. Often their jobs were based on women's traditional work such as cooking, housekeeping, caring for visitors and sick people, and providing company for men. Women brewed ale, prepared food, ran inns, took in boarders, worked as nurses, cleaners, servants, barmaids and entertainers. All these women's jobs had low status and were badly paid. Towns were also home to many abandoned women, who came there to beg, or to look for work.

A woman dancer balances on the shoulders of her partner. Women dancers, musicians, acrobats and jugglers entertained ordinary people on festival days and at town fairs and markets.

From farm to market

By about 1300 most peasants went to market every week, in their nearest large village or town. They sold home-produced food, such as vegetables or eggs. Some women set up take-out food stalls. Others built up larger businesses, selling goods they had bought from craftworkers or merchants. Some even worked as moneylenders. Women traders had a reputation for driving a hard bargain. One English writer stated, "But, to tell the truth, the retail shopkeeping trade belongs most rightly to women.... A woman will never give up the profit from a single crumb.... It is a waste of time to beg her for anything, since she does nothing from goodness of heart."

In this picture (below) women are selling bread, fruit and vegetables at a market. Most food selling was managed by women.

Noblewomen

Compared with peasant women and girls, rich noblewomen led sheltered, comfortable lives. But they were not idle. They needed just as many management skills as the head of a large company today.

Young noblewomen have a snowball fight outside the walls of their castle.

Women in charge

Noblewomen might be in charge of hundreds of servants, including cooks, chambermaids, grooms, gardeners and bodyguards. They gave orders, settled quarrels, listened to complaints, and hired and fired staff. They ordered new linen, tapestries and furniture, so that visitors were impressed by the family's wealth, and sometimes managed whole estates, or defended houses or castles from attack, while husbands were away.

Vital skills

To manage all these tasks, a noblewoman needed to be a clever judge of character. She had to know which members of the household were hard-working and loyal, and which only wanted to make use of her family's rank and wealth for their own ambition. She also had to be able to read, to write (or dictate) business letters, and to do accounts. For this, she might have male scribes and secretaries to help her, as well as female domestic staff.

A noblewoman hands a letter to a messenger. After about 1300, many noblewomen could read and write. They used these skills to manage their estates.

32

ntertaining and politics

...noblewoman had to be diplomatic.
...was her duty to entertain visitors, some
...portant and powerful, in a way that
...ought honor to her family. Her early
...ining in correct behavior (see page 11)
...lped her, but she also needed a gracious
...nner, a good memory, a lively wit, and
...-to-date information about politics.

...urnaments were mock battles, where men
...ught to win fame. Women were expected to
...end them, to bring honor to their families
...being charming and beautifully dressed.

...ace—and power struggles

...en before the Middle Ages, noblewomen
...re famous as peacemakers, using their
...mmon sense and wisdom to settle quarrels.
...dieval women continued this pattern,
...ilding networks of friends and allies in
...al communities and at the royal court.
...ey could also be aggressive, fiercely
...hting legal battles, spreading rumors,
...bribing supporters, to help their family
...in more land or win power.

...'s funeral statue shows Queen Philippa in old
...e. Legally she had no power, but she often
...luenced her husband's actions.

QUEEN PHILIPPA BEGS FOR MERCY

During the Hundred Years War (1337–1453) between England and France, English soldiers surrounded the city of Calais. After a siege, the French were forced to surrender. King Edward III of England planned to execute six leading citizens of Calais, to punish the city for fighting against him. But Queen Philippa, his wife, who was born near Calais, took pity on them. The fourteenth-century writer quoted below describes Philippa as extremely pregnant to stress the queen's female role.

Then noble Queen Philippa of England, who was extremely pregnant, begged King Edward to be merciful. She did this so gently and graciously that he could not refuse her. The good, noble queen kneeled on the ground before her husband and master, and said, ".... I humbly beg you to grant me a favor, for Jesus' sake, and because you love me. Please pardon these six men."

WOMEN AND RELIGION

Married to God

Women had little power in the Christian Church. All Church leaders were men. Men made religious laws and wrote most religious books. Yet many women wanted to lead a religious life. So they became nuns, living in religious communities, away from family and friends. They were described as being married to God.

Nuns usually taught children, but a few learned women gained great respect as teachers. Here an abbess teaches a young nobleman.

Who could become a nun?

In theory, all women could become nuns. But many religious communities demanded a dowry. This meant that only women from wealthy families could join. Poor women worked as servants to the nuns. Toward the end of the Middle Ages, many more small religious communities for ordinary women were set up in villages and towns.

> *I saw, gathered together, many holy virgins. They turned away from the delights and riches of this world, to prepare themselves for the kingdom of heaven. They lived humbly for the sake of their heavenly husband [God], and earned a simple living by working hard at everyday tasks....*
>
> JACQUES DE VITRY (1180–1240),
> A LEADING FRENCH CHURCHMAN

Learning and nursing

A few women became nuns to escape arranged marriages. Others wanted to study or teach. Nuns were the best-educated women in Europe. They kept libraries, copied manuscripts, wrote religious and medical books, and ran schools. Many parents gave their daughters to the Church (see box). They hoped to help their families by forming a link with God. Older women retired to nunneries after their children had grown up or their husbands had died.

Some groups of nuns set up hospitals to care for the sick. Here nuns are supervising the care of patients at the Hôtel Dieu in Paris, one of the most famous hospitals in Europe.

oldiers were not supposed to attack nuns. But in
artime, abbeys were tempting places, with gold
d silver crosses and food supplies. Here a nun
shown protecting her abbey from a soldier.

way of life

took several years of training to become
nun. Novices (trainees) studied religious
owledge, learned to sing hymns and say
ayers, and joined in the work of the
ligious community. When they were fully
ained they made religious promises (called
ws) of poverty, chastity and obedience.
om then on, they lived by the community's
les. There was a strict routine of up to
even church services a day, with time for
ading, working and sleeping.

HILDEGARD OF BINGEN
(1098–1179)

Hildegard was born into a noble family
in Germany. Her parents decided that
she should become a nun, and sent her
away at the age of eight to live with an
aunt, who was an anchoress (see page
36). Other women came to join her, and
a nunnery was built to house them.
In 1136 Hildegard became its abbess.
At about the same time, she also began
to write religious books and medical
texts, music, poetry and plays.

From childhood, Hildegard had religious
visions. She wrote about them in her
books, and they inspired people with
their beauty and power. In one vision,
Hildegard described herself as "a feather
[floating] on the breath of God."

*This medieval painting illustrates Hildegard's
description of how people should know and
love God. It shows her at the center of a
circle. The circle represents God the Father,
his son Jesus Christ, and the Holy Spirit, sent
by God to guide humans after Jesus died.*

Alone with God

Many women felt that living in a religious community was not the best way to find God. They did not want to be surrounded by nuns, or have to follow strict rules all the time. Instead, they shut themselves away from the world, and lived alone, praying and meditating about God.

Anchoresses were shut away from the world forever in a special ceremony. Here a bishop blesses an anchoress who has just taken her vows. All we can see is her face, peering out of the window in a small churchlike building, where she will live for the rest of her life.

Place your mind before the mirror of eternity!
Place your soul in the brilliance of glory!
So that you too may feel what His [Jesus'] friends feel as they taste the hidden sweetness which God has reserved from the beginning for those who love Him.

FROM A LETTER WRITTEN BY ST. CLARE OF ASSISI (C. 1193–1253) TO A CZECH PRINCESS

Locked away

A woman who locked herself away, dedicating her life to God, was called an anchoress. Anchoresses usually lived in rooms at the side of a church. The doors were locked and the windows were barred, like a prison cell. Some anchoresses, such as Julian of Norwich (see box), gave spiritual advice to visitors, or taught religion to children. Others saw no one except priests and the servants who brought them food and water every day.

Dead to the world

It was not easy to become an anchoress. Church leaders carefully questioned the women to make sure that their faith was strong and to make them think very hard about what they were doing. Then, in a special religious ceremony, they were locked away from the world. The ceremony contained well-known prayers for the dead. A new anchoress was also sprinkled with earth as she entered her cell, as a sign of burial. In the eyes of the Church, anchoresses were "dead and buried to the world."

A respected role

Both men and women could shut themselves away. But for women the decision had a special meaning. For the first time, it gave them control of their own lives. It also brought them respect from the rest of the community. Medieval people believed that by saying prayers, anchoresses were doing important work to help everyone else.

Visions of God

Many religious women were mystics. They had vivid religious experiences in trances or dreams. Many believed that they saw, or even spoke to, God. Like St. Clare of Assisi, they described these visions as full of sweetness and glory. They wrote about this holy joy in books or letters to their friends.

St. Clare of Assisi ran away from home to become a nun. She founded a community with other women who shared her belief in a life of poverty and long hours of praying.

JULIAN OF NORWICH
(c. 1342–c. 1429)

Julian was an anchoress at a church in Norwich, in eastern England. We know little about her life. When she was about 30 years old, she became very ill, and during her illness she had many visions. She spent the rest of her life praying and meditating about their meaning, and described them in a book. Julian's message was that people should trust in God's love. She was one of the earliest writers to describe Jesus as "our sweet, kind, and ever-loving mother." This made a striking change from the usual image of God as an all-powerful father.

This picture shows St. Brigitta of Sweden. All her life she had visions, which she believed came from God. Here she is shown listening to holy words whispered in her ear by an angel.

Private Worship

Although some women shut themselves away and devoted their lives to God, most medieval women could not do this. Whether they were rich or poor, most women had to marry and look after their families.

Religion and daily life

Religious teachers taught ordinary women to combine religious activities with their day-to-day work. We do not know exactly how many women followed this advice but, compared with today, many women, rich and poor, did give a great deal of time and thought to religion. Some, such as Margery Kempe (see box), won both praise and blame for their religious behavior.

She gets up at 7 AM, and her chaplain [private priest] is waiting to say morning prayers ... and when she has washed and dressed, she listens to another service in her room, and then she has breakfast, then she goes to the chapel, for another service, then has dinner, during which she listens to readings from holy books. After dinner, she discusses business ... then has a short sleep, then says her prayers, then drinks ale or wine. Then, her chaplain says evening prayers, after which she goes to the chapel for evening service, and has supper. After supper, she relaxes with her women attendants, and takes a cup of wine. After that, she goes to her private room, and says nighttime prayers. By 8 PM she is in bed.

DESCRIPTION OF THE DAILY ROUTINE OF CICELY, DUCHESS OF YORK (1415–1495)

Priests and prayer books

Women brought religion into their everyday lives in many ways. Ordinary women visited their local church to say prayers. Cicely of York, a rich noblewoman (see quotation), could afford to pay for a private priest to live in her household and hold services for her. Most castles and manor houses had private chapels, where noblewomen could pray. Rich women could also afford to pay for religious books, such as collections of prayers or the lives of saints. In their wills they often gave orders for carved and painted tombs to be made for them. These were memorials to themselves and families, but they also sent out a religious message to anyone who saw them.

A woman kneels in front of a priest to confess her sins and ask God to forgive her. This image comes from a length of silk patterned with scenes from women's religious life, made in 1500.

This stained glass window tells the story of Ruth, from the Bible. She was seen as an example of a faithful woman. Women praying in church saw pictures like this and were inspired by them.

Giving to charity

The Christian Church taught that giving to charity was very important. Historians think that women often gave more money or practical help to the poor and sick than men did. Rich women gave large amounts of land to help pay for new churches, schools and colleges. Ordinary women gave food and clothing to beggars, the sick and the old.

Women as well as men went on pilgrimages to holy sites. Pilgrimages could be solemn, or they could be cheerful, and almost like a vacation.

MARGERY KEMPE
(born *c.* 1373)

Margery Kempe came from a rich family in a busy town in Norfolk, England. She married young, ran a business, and had 14 children. But while she was still quite young, Margery decided that she would like to lead a religious life.

She spent many years persuading her husband to let her live alone, and finally he agreed. She traveled to holy sites, such as Jerusalem and Rome. Wherever she went, Margery spoke out about her religious experiences, and often fell down, weeping with religious emotion. Church leaders accused her of being a member of a radical religious movement where women were equal with men. They threatened her, but she refused to stay silent.

Toward the end of her life, Margery dictated her story to two priests. It still survives, and gives us a vivid picture of her strong character, as well as of her struggle to live a religious life in the everyday world.

Pilgrimage

If they could find the time, rich and poor women liked to go on pilgrimages. They visited holy places where saints had been buried or where miracles had occurred. Toward the end of the Middle Ages, pilgrimage sites linked to the Virgin Mary were especially popular. Some pilgrim routes were safe, with overnight stops at comfortable inns. Others could be rough and dangerous. Pilgrims faced attack from bandits or wild animals.

Saints and Sinners

The Church, the law, and many medieval writers assumed that women were naturally more wicked than men, and that it was man's duty to control them. They believed that bad behavior was a danger to the wicked woman's soul, and would bring shame to her family, too. Good or bad, women were always judged, praised or punished by men.

Gossip and rumors

Many crimes that women were accused of were, by today's standards, hardly crimes at all. Women were often accused of vanity, which was seen as one of the seven most deadly sins. Women were accused of gossiping and spreading rumors more than men. They might be accused of making friends that their husbands did not approve of, of swearing, and of being lazy. A woman who slept with another man was punished severely. In Italy, for example, she was beaten in public and then exiled. If a man slept with another woman, he was not usually punished.

Desperate crimes

From records of medieval law courts, we know that women's most common crime was petty theft. This included stealing leftover stalks of wheat from the fields at harvest time and taking food, animals or other salable goods from people's homes. Most of these thefts occurred because women were desperate to provide food and warmth for their families, but they were still punished.

This illustration shows a priest and a woman, with their legs locked in a wooden trap called the stocks. Men and women were put in the stocks to punish bad behavior. Offenders had to sit in public view, while passers-by laughed at them, and even threw rotten food.

40

...is painting is one of a series about sin.
...e artist has shown the sin of vanity as a
...oman. She is admiring herself in a mirror,
...hich is held up by a devil.

...aintly behavior

...lale Church leaders, and many other
...nedieval men, admired the self-sacrificing
...nd dedicated behavior of women saints.
...ut these women, such as St. Elizabeth of
...lungary (see box), were always exceptional.
...heir behavior was often odd, and
...ometimes extreme. They saw visions, fainted
...nd fell into trances. Many had eating
...isorders. Some, such as St. Zita of Lucca,
...eliberately scratched their faces to make
...ure no man would approach them. Others,
...uch as St. Clare of Assisi, developed marks
...n their bodies exactly like Jesus Christ's
...ounds on the cross.

This painting is an
imaginary portrait of
St. Elizabeth of Hungary,
painted about 50 years
after she died. The
artist has shown her
as humble and
obedient to God.

41

Women with Power

Eleanor of Aquitaine

How could women in medieval Europe win fame in public life? Some persuaded men to do what they wanted. Others acted as deputies while their husbands were away. Most women, no matter how skilled or clever, used the position of their fathers, husbands or sons to gain power.

AELFGIFU (C. 1000–C. 1040)

Aelfgifu was the daughter of an Anglo-Saxon nobleman. She became the concubine of King Cnut of Denmark, who ruled most of Scandinavia and the British Isles from 1016 to 1035. Cnut and Aelfgifu had two sons, Sweyn and Harold "Harefoot." While Cnut was away fighting, he made Aelfgifu the ruler until Sweyn grew up. Aelfgifu was unpopular in Norway, and many stories were told about her cruelty. When Cnut died, the Norwegians drove her out of the country. She returned to England, and by 1037 had persuaded the English to accept her other son, Harold, as king. After Harold's death in 1040, Aelfgifu's name does not appear in any documents, from England or Norway. Historians think that she may have died, or been killed, at about this time.

Aelfgifu and King Cnut give a cross to a church.

ELEANOR OF AQUITAINE (1122–1204)

Eleanor was the wife of King Louis VII of France. She advised the king on many political issues, and even went with him on a Crusade, taking 300 servants with her to care for the wounded. Louis and Eleanor had two daughters, but Louis wanted a son. He was also angry at Eleanor's friendship with other powerful men. He ended their marriage in 1152. Eleanor kept control of her lands, and married Prince Henry of England. In England Eleanor joined in plots led by her sons against their father. King Henry put her in prison, where she stayed until he died in 1189. When her son Richard the Lionheart became king, she ruled for him while he was abroad.

Eleanor was also a patron of learning. She entertained writers, scholars, musicians and artists, and founded many schools and churches in France. When she was 79 she went to a nunnery, where she died the following year.

BLANCHE OF CASTILE (1188–1252)

Blanche was a Spanish princess. At the age of 12 she was married to King Louis VIII of France. She helped him plan wars and rule France. When Louis died in 1226, their son was only 12, so Blanche ruled France for the next eight years. This was not an easy task. French nobles rebelled against her, but she led an army against them, riding into battle on a white horse. She also expanded the area ruled by France by making peace treaties and marriage alliances. When her son Louis IX took over the government, Blanche continued to advise him. When Louis went on a Crusade, in 1248, his mother ran France until her death four years later.

Queen Blanche of Castile at prayer.

JOAN OF ARC (C. 1412–1431)

Joan was a French peasant girl who saw visions of Christian saints. She believed they were telling her to lead French soldiers to fight against the British. The Church and army leaders gave her men's clothes, weapons and a horse, and she led French troops to victory against the English. But soon afterward she was captured and sold to the English. She was put on trial as a witch, and for holding false beliefs, and was executed. She was made a saint in 1920 and is now seen as a brave heroine.

MARGARET OF ANJOU (1430–1482)

Margaret was a French princess. At 15 she was married to King Henry VI of England as part of a peace treaty between England and France. Margaret was beautiful and intelligent; Henry was sickly and devoted to religion. Soon Margaret took over many of her husband's government duties. Margaret plotted against rivals for the throne, but was defeated in battle and forced to flee for her life. She spent two years on the run in disguise before reaching France. In 1471 her allies won power in England, and she returned to London. But there was more fighting. Her son was killed in battle, Henry VI died and Margaret was put in prison. In 1476 she returned to France, where she died in poverty.

ISABELLA OF CASTILE (1451–1504)

Isabella was the daughter of King Juan of Castile (the northern part of Spain). Her mother helped her gain acceptance as the heir to her father's throne. Despite opposition, she chose her own husband, Prince Ferdinand of Aragon, who ruled the southern half of Spain. Under their rule, Spain became a united country for the first time. Even so, Isabella insisted on ruling Castile by herself. She changed the government and laws, founded new schools, encouraged scholars, artists and musicians, and gave money to pay for Christopher Columbus's voyages of exploration. But she was strongly criticized, even at the time, for her religious intolerance, especially for driving Jews and Muslims out of Spain.

Joan of Arc, wearing armor and carrying a sword, ready to fight for France against the English.

Learned Ladies

Most medieval scholars were men, and most thought that women's minds were too weak for them to be good at studying. Most schools and all universities refused to admit women students. The Church taught that it was sinful for women to teach or speak in public, especially on religious topics. In spite of this, some medieval women proved that they could study as well as men. These women were mostly nuns, or wealthy nobles who had the money to pay teachers and buy books, and had time to study.

Heloise leaving Abelard to go to the nunnery.

HELOISE (1101–1164)

Heloise came from a rich family in France. Her uncle saw that she was eager to learn and asked Abelard, a young scholar at the University of Paris, to teach Heloise at home. Abelard and Heloise fell in love. This caused terrible problems because Abelard was a priest as well as a scholar, and was not allowed by Church law to marry. But Heloise became pregnant and had a son, and ran away to marry Abelard. In response, Heloise's uncle had Abelard captured and punished. Full of regret, Abelard decided to spend the rest of his life as a monk, and persuaded Heloise to become a nun. She was very unhappy, but continued to study and also ran the nunnery. The nunnery became one of the most famous for learning in France. Twelve years later someone gave Heloise a copy of Abelard's autobiography. This reawakened her love, and she wrote him a series of passionate letters. Abelard wrote back, urging her to seek only God's love. They continued to write—but only about philosophy and religion.

FATIMA OF CORDOBA (C. 1000)

Fatima lived in the city of Cordoba, capital of Muslim Spain. The rulers there had the largest library in Europe. Fatima was employed by them as a senior member of the library staff, along with other women librarians, copyists (who copied manuscripts by hand) and scribes. Fatima's task was to buy new books and manuscripts from all over the world. This meant that she had to have a wide knowledge of many subjects. Muslim scholars were experts in philosophy, science, medicine, geography, astronomy and math. The rulers trusted her so much that they gave her unlimited money to spend. Fatima met and wrote to male scholars from many distant lands. But like other women scholars she never married. She had to choose between a family and a career.

The library at Cordoba collected manuscripts from all over the Muslim world.

44

NOVELLA D'ANDREA (DIED 1333)

Novella was the daughter of a professor of law in Italy. She studied with her father and was so intelligent that she gave lectures in his place while he was away. People said that she sat behind a curtain to teach, so that students (all men) would not be distracted from their studies by her beauty. She married another scholar, but died while still young.

A statue of Lady Margaret stands over the gateway at Trinity College, Cambridge.

CHRISTINE DE PISAN (1364–1430)

Christine was the daughter of an Italian scholar who served the king of France as astrologer and physician. She grew up in France and married a French courtier when she was 15. He died 10 years later and Christine decided to earn her living as a writer. She wrote the kinds of books she knew would please rich people at the French court—history, poetry and biography. Christine's books were entertaining, but some of them had a serious side. She was one of the first female writers to discuss the role of women in society, how they were treated, and what they were capable of. She wrote books about famous women who had lived in the past and defended women from the attacks of male writers, claiming that women were more reliable and generous than men. when she was about 50, she retired to a convent. Her last known work is a poem about Joan of Arc.

LADY MARGARET BEAUFORT (1443–1509)

Lady Margaret was a member of a powerful English family. Her mother gave her a good education, but Margaret did not have much time to study. She was married at 12, widowed at 13, and then married twice more, to noblemen with political ambitions—which she shared. In 1485, once her son had become Henry VII of England, Margaret gave up politics for a life of religion, scholarship and charity. She was interested in printing, the most exciting new technology of her day, and sponsored two printing presses. Thanks to this, new books and new ideas became more widely available to scholars in Britain, and to people studying at home. Toward the end of her life, Margaret took religious vows, and spent most of her time in prayer and study in her own palace. When she died, she left most of her fortune to colleges at Cambridge University.

HROSTWITHA (C. AD 935–972)

Hrostwitha was a member of a noble German family. She left home to become a nun, and also became famous as the first woman in Europe to write plays. She wrote mostly in Latin, on religious themes. Her best-known plays told the true stories of women who died bravely rather than give up their Christian faith. She also wrote poems and histories.

Christine de Pisan on her knees, offering a book to Queen Isabella of France.

GLOSSARY

abbess A woman leader of a community of nuns.

accounts Written records of money earned and spent.

alliance An agreement between people or nations.

allies Nations that agree to help one another.

astrologer Someone who studies the movement of the stars and planets, and relates this knowledge to people's characters and actions.

chapel A small church where Christian people pray.

Celts Peoples who lived in northern Europe from about 800 BC to AD 100. Traces of their civilization survived until medieval times.

ceremony A gathering of people, with music, processions and sometimes prayers, held in honor of a special event.

Christian Church (also, the Church) The most important religious organization in medieval Europe, made up of people who believed in the religious teachings of Jesus Christ. The Church was wealthy, and controlled most schools and universities.

citizen A person who lives in a city or country and has rights as a member of the community there.

coat of arms A painted badge first worn worn by noble soldiers to identify themselves in battle. Soon it became a sign of high rank.

concubine An unmarried woman who lives with a married man.

contract A legal agreement.

dedicate To give something (from a book to one's own life) wholly to a person, or a cause, or to God.

devote To give time and love to.

dictate Speak words out loud while someone else writes them down.

diplomatic Politically tactful.

document A written record.

dower A share of family property given to a widow when her husband died.

dowry Money and property given by a bride's family to a bridegroom's family on marriage.

estate Land including its houses, fields and farms.

flax A tall plant. Fibers from its stalks are woven to make linen cloth.

garland A necklace or crown of flowers.

girdle A type of belt, made of leather or cloth.

guardian A person who is legally responsible for looking after someone else.

guild A group of workers who join together to keep high standards of work and to help one another.

homespun Rough cloth woven at home.

immoral Breaking society's laws of good behavior

inherit To receive goods or land when someone dies.

kerchief A piece of cloth worn on the head or neck.

manuscript A document written by hand, sometimes decorated with paintings.

marriage alliance A friendly agreement between families linked by marriage.

meditate To think deeply about important things.

memorial A work of art made to help people remember someone who has died.

merchant A person who makes a living by buying and selling goods.

midwife A woman trained to help mothers in childbirth.

noble A person of high rank.

official A person who works for a government or other large organization.

pagan A person who does not believe in the Christian, Jewish or Muslim God.

peace treaty An agreement to end a war.

peasants People who survive by growing their own food and raising their own animals.

pilgrimage A journey to a holy place.

priest A man trained by the Christian Church to lead worship and offer spiritual advice.

rank A person's position in society.

remedy A medicine or other cure for a disease.

romance A medieval love story.

Romans People who lived in an empire, ruled from Rome, Italy, from about 800 BC to 500 AD.

saints' days Festival days throughout the year when Christian saints were remembered and honored.

salt To preserve food by packing it in layers of salt.

scholar A person who studies hard.

scribe A person trained to keep written records.

shift A long, loose shirt, worn by women.

siege When a town or castle is surrounded by soldiers trying to capture it.

Slavs Peoples who live in eastern Europe.

tax Money collected by the government to pay for public services, such as the army or road building.

trance A state where someone seems to be asleep even though they are still awake.

Vikings People who lived in Scandinavia from about AD 800 to 1100. They traveled, raided and settled in many parts of western Europe.

vision A waking dream.

water mill A machine for grinding grain into flour, powered by fast-flowing water.

wet nurse A servant who breastfeeds another woman's baby.

FURTHER READING

Laurie Carlson, *Days of Knights and Damsels: An Activity Guide* (Chicago Review Press, 1998)
Karen Cushman & Trina Schart Hyman, *The Midwife's Apprentice* (Clarion Books, 1995)
Vicki Leon, *Outrageous Women of the Middle Ages* (Wiley, 1998)

INDEX